Coloring Book for Adults (and Big Kids!) for Anti-Stress and Relaxation

Beautiful Abstract Patterns and Intricate Ornate Tile Designs

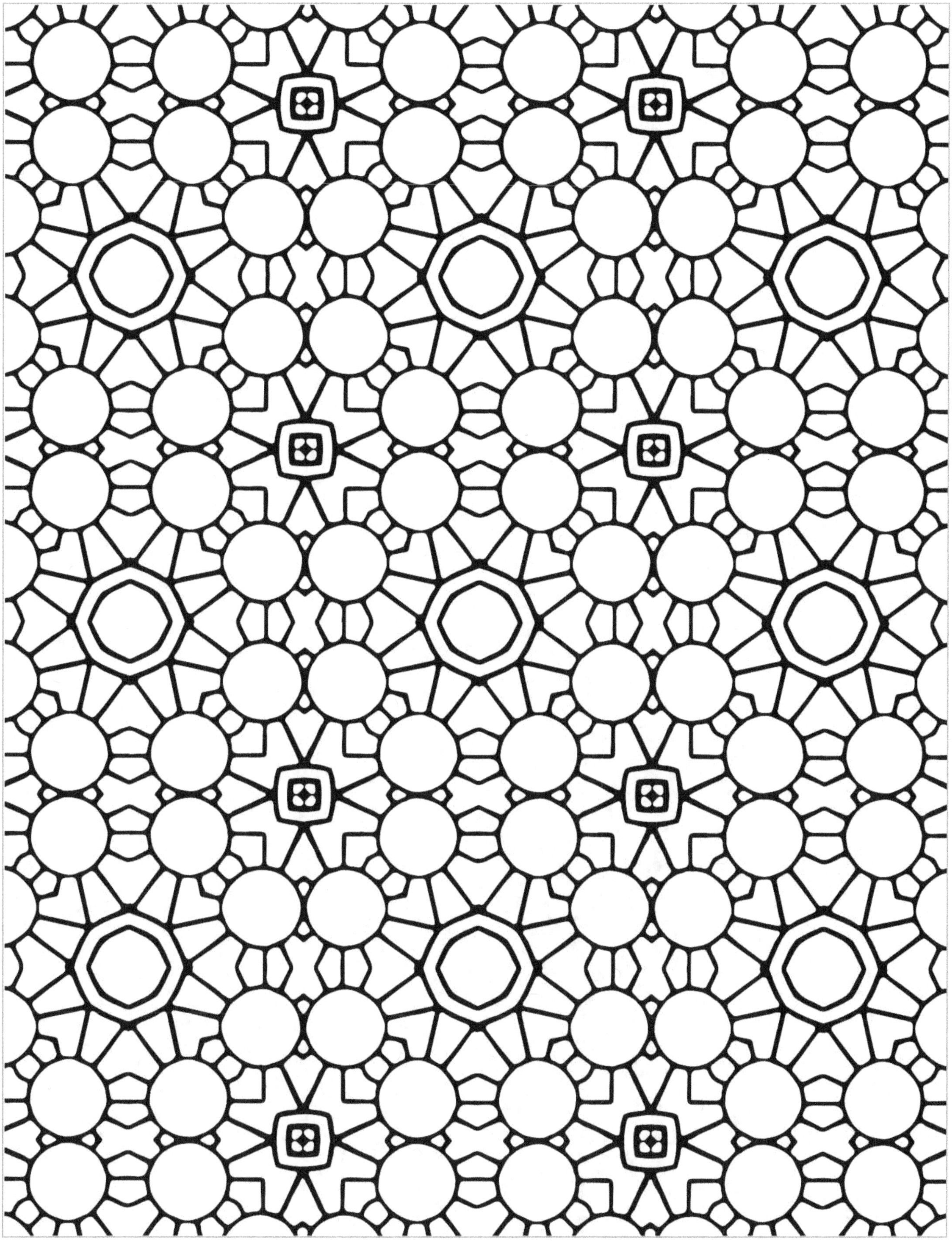

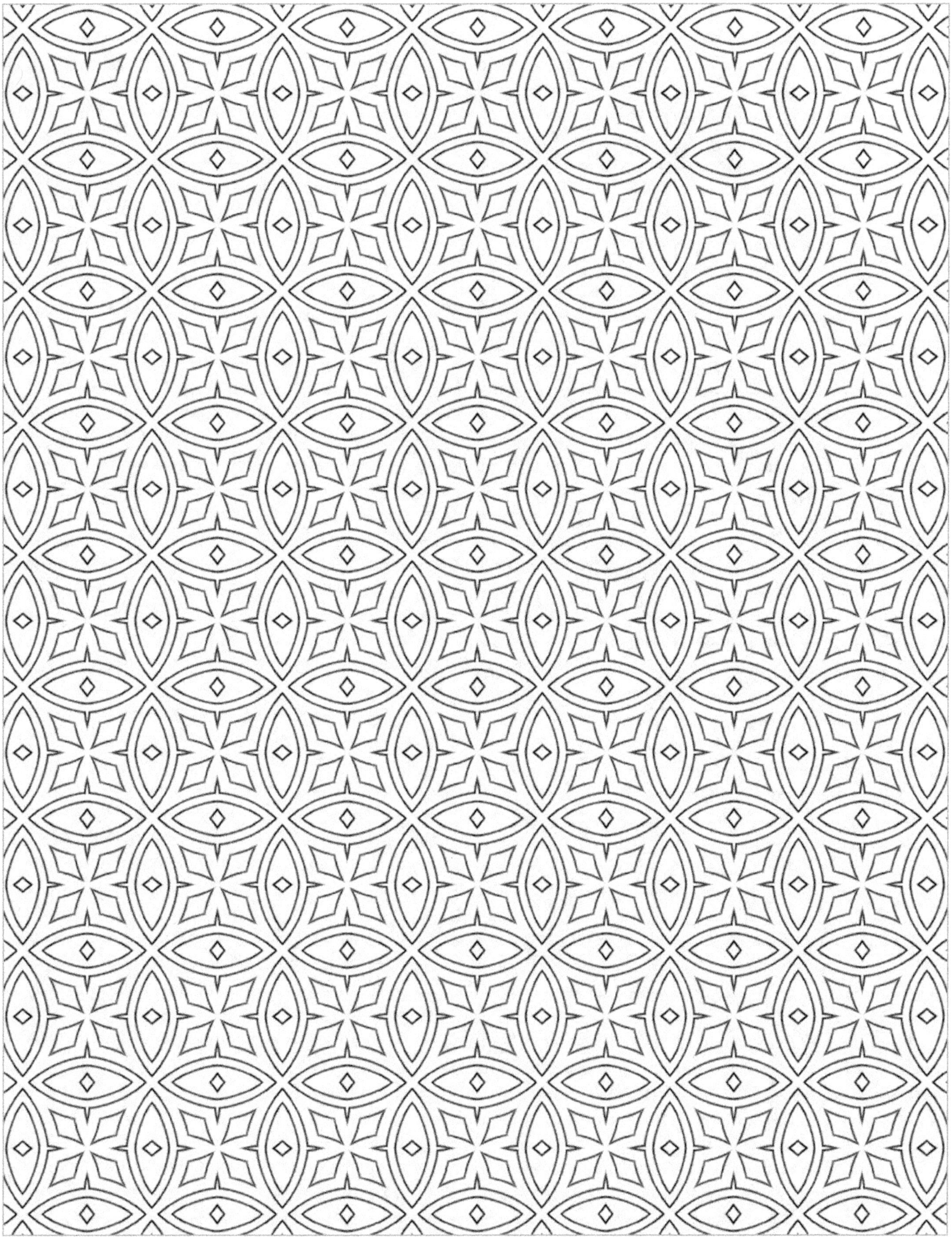

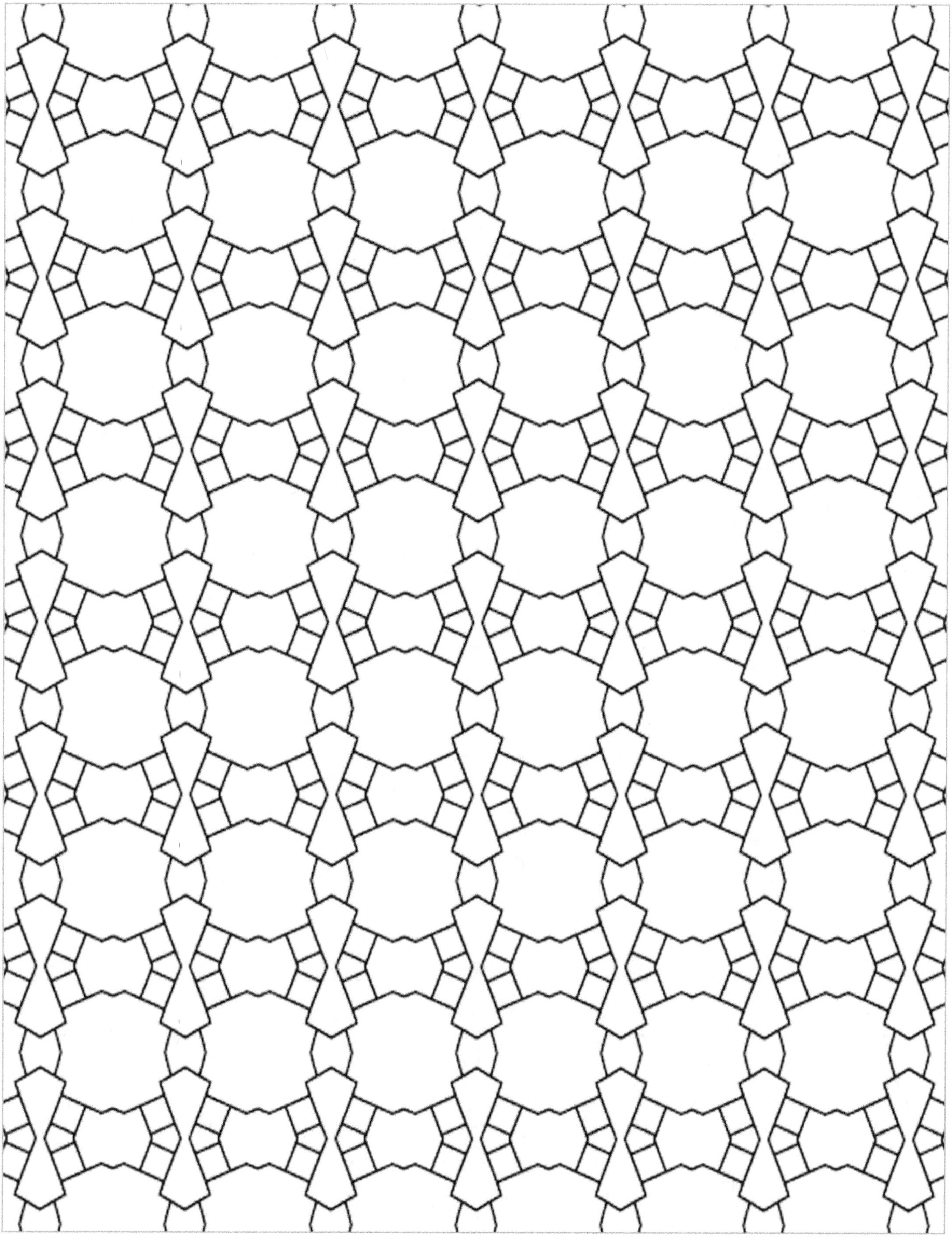

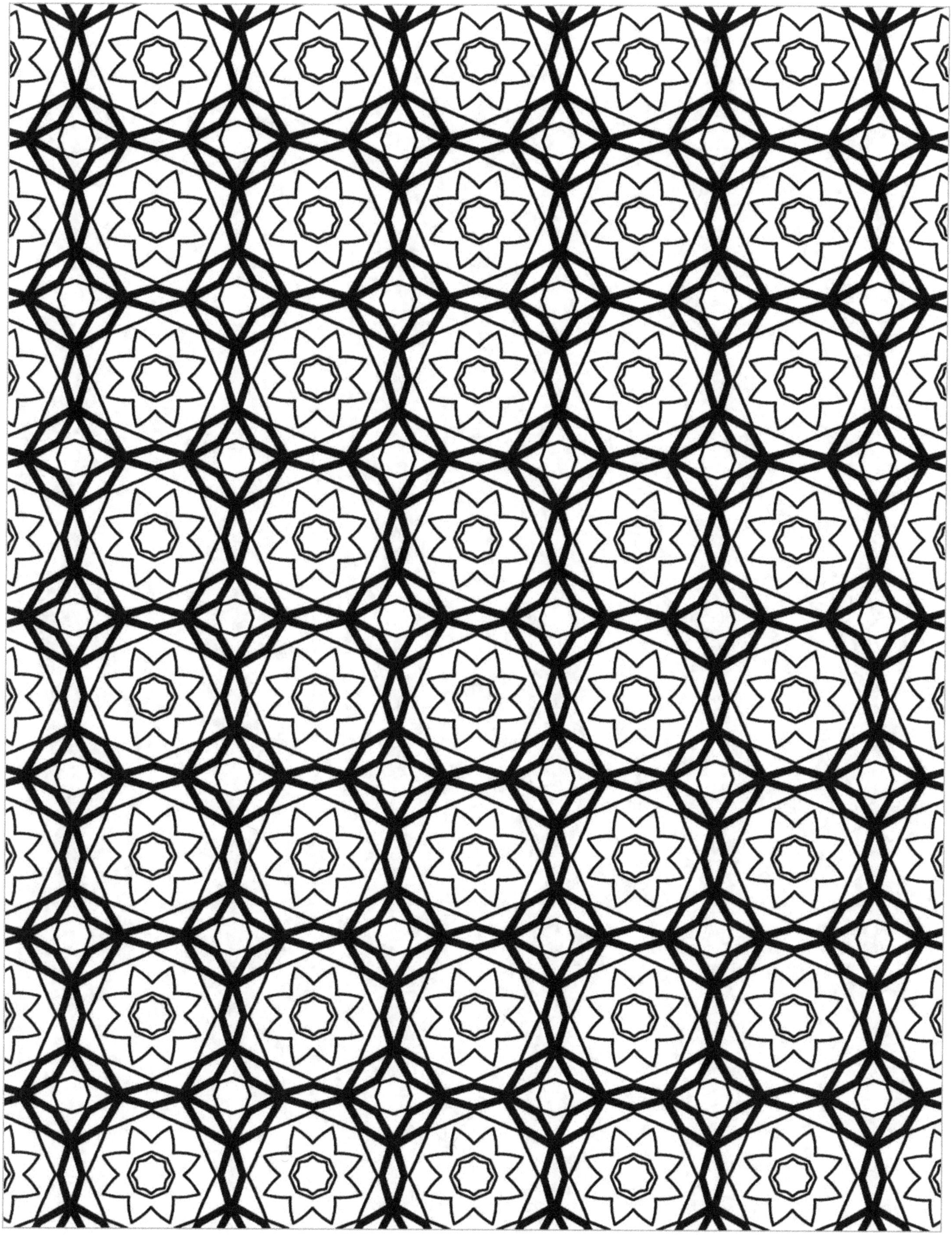

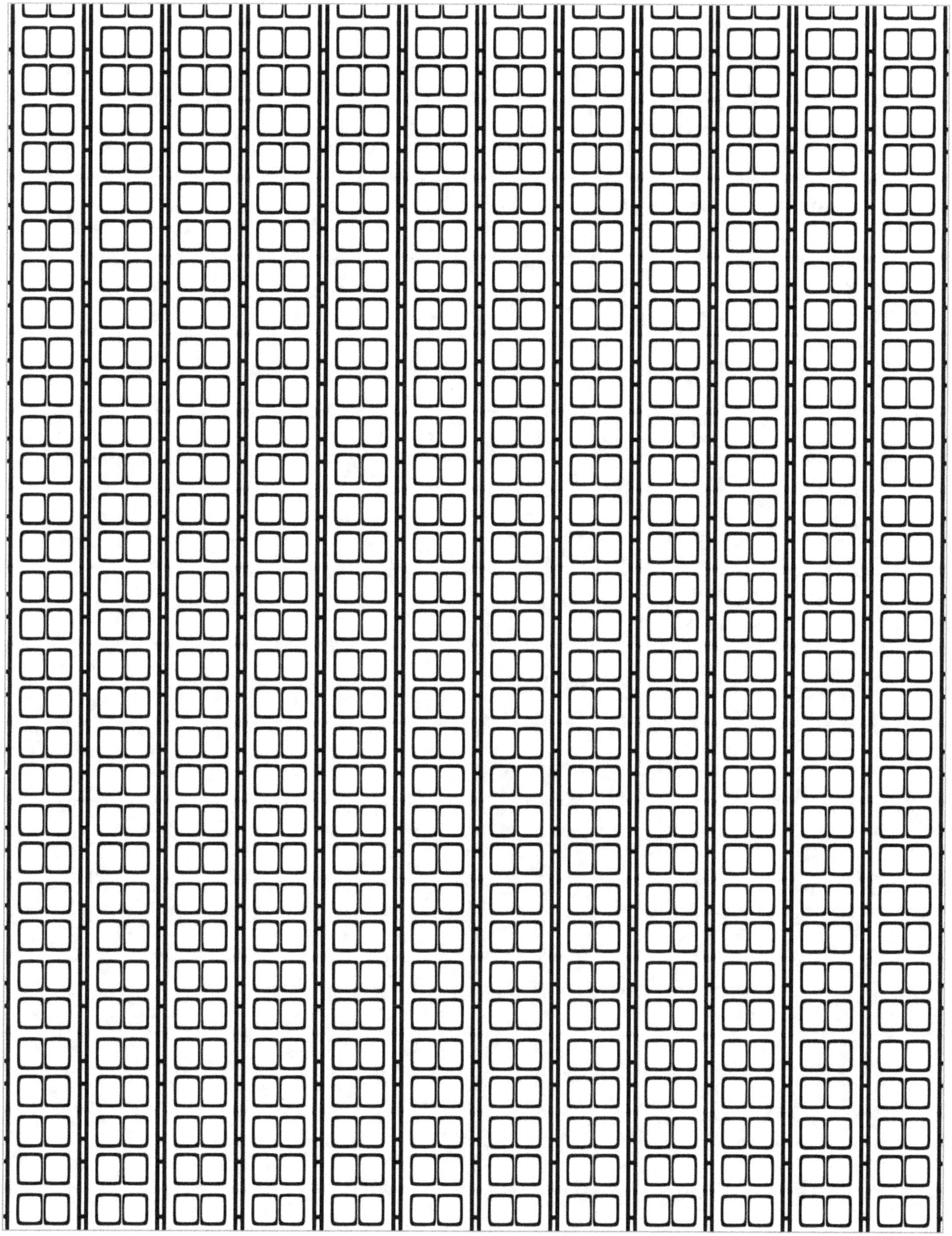

www.ingramcontent.com/pod-product-compliance
Lightning Source LLC
Chambersburg PA
CBHW080430290526
45791CB00008BA/2447